United States Government Accountability Office

GAO

Report to the Ranking Member,
Committee on Homeland Security, House
of Representatives

July 2012

SECURITY CLEARANCES

Agencies Need Clearly Defined Policy for Determining Civilian Position Requirements

GAO

Accountability ★ Integrity ★ Reliability

GAO-12-800

SECURITY CLEARANCES

Agencies Need Clearly Defined Policy for Determining Civilian Position Requirements

Highlights of GAO-12-800, a report to the Ranking Member, Committee on Homeland Security, House of Representatives

Why GAO Did This Study

Security clearances allow personnel access to classified information that, through unauthorized disclosure, can, in some cases, cause exceptionally grave damage to U.S. national security. In 2011, the DNI reported that over 4.8 million federal government and contractor employees held or were eligible for a clearance. To safeguard classified data and manage costs, agencies need an effective process to determine whether civilian positions require a clearance. GAO was asked to examine the extent to which the executive branch has established policies and procedures for agencies to use when (1) first determining if federal civilian positions require a security clearance and (2) reviewing and revising or validating existing federal civilian position security clearance requirements. GAO reviewed executive orders and the Code of Federal Regulations and met with officials from ODNI and OPM because of their Directors' assigned roles as Security and Suitability executive agents, as well as DHS and DOD based on the volume of clearances they process.

What GAO Recommends

GAO recommends that the DNI issue clearly defined policy for agencies to follow when determining if federal civilian positions require a security clearance, and that the DNI and Director of OPM collaborate to revise the existing position designation tool. GAO further recommends that the DNI issue guidance to require agencies to periodically review and revise or validate the designation of their existing federal civilian positions. ODNI and OPM concurred, although OPM raised concerns with which GAO disagrees and addresses in the report.

View GAO-12-800. For more information, contact Brenda S. Farrell at (202) 512-3604 or farrellb@gao.gov

What GAO Found

The Director of National Intelligence (DNI), as Security Executive Agent, has not provided agencies clearly defined policy and procedures to consistently determine if a position requires a security clearance. Executive Order 13467 assigns DNI responsibility for, among other things, developing uniform and consistent policies to determine eligibility for access to classified information, and gives the DNI authority to issue guidance to agency heads to ensure uniformity in processes relating to those determinations. In the absence of this guidance, agencies are using an Office of Personnel Management (OPM) tool that OPM designed to determine the sensitivity and risk levels of civilian positions which, in turn, inform the type of investigation needed. OPM audits, however, found inconsistency in these position designations, and some agencies described problems in implementing OPM's tool. In an April 2012 audit, OPM reviewed the sensitivity levels of 39 positions in an agency within the Department of Defense (DOD) and reached different conclusions than the agency for 26 of them. Problems exist, in part, because OPM and the Office of the Director of National Intelligence (ODNI) did not collaborate on the development of the position designation tool, and because their roles for suitability—consideration of character and conduct for federal employment—and security clearance reform are still evolving. Without guidance from the DNI, and without collaboration between the DNI and OPM in future revisions to the tool, executive branch agencies will continue to risk making security clearance determinations that are inconsistent or at improper levels.

The DNI also has not established guidance to require agencies to review and revise or validate existing federal civilian position designations. Executive Order 12968 says each agency shall request or grant clearance determinations, subject to certain exceptions, based on a demonstrated need for access, and keep to a minimum the number of employees that it determines are eligible for access to classified information. The order also states that access to classified information shall be terminated when an employee no longer has a need for access, and prohibits agencies from requesting or approving eligibility in excess of actual requirements for access. During this review of Department of Homeland Security (DHS) and DOD components, GAO found that agency officials were aware of the need to keep the number of security clearances to a minimum, but were not always required to conduct periodic reviews and validations of the security clearance needs of existing positions. Overdesignating positions results in significant cost implications, given that the fiscal year 2012 base price for a top secret clearance investigation conducted by OPM is $4,005, while the base price of a secret clearance is $260. Conversely, underdesignating positions could lead to security risks. GAO found that the agencies follow varying practices because the DNI has not established guidance that requires executive branch agencies to review and revise or validate position designations on a recurring basis. Without such a requirement, executive branch agencies may be hiring and budgeting for initial and periodic security clearance investigations using position descriptions and security clearance requirements that no longer reflect national security needs. Further, since reviews are not done consistently, DHS and DOD and other executive branch agencies cannot have assurances that they are keeping the number of positions that require security clearances to a minimum.

_____ **United States Government Accountability Office**

Contents

Tables

Figures

Abbreviations

Office of the Director of National Intelligence (ODNI)
Department of Defense (DOD)
Department of Homeland Security (DHS)
Office of Personnel Management (OPM)
Single Scope Background Investigation (SSBI)
Access National Agency Check and Inquiries (ANACI)
Moderate Risk Background Investigation (MBI)
Intelligence Reform and Terrorism Prevention Act of 2004 (IRTPA)
Director of National Intelligence (DNI)
Office of Management and Budget (OMB)
Sensitive Compartmented Information (SCI)

United States Government Accountability Office
Washington, DC 20548

July 12, 2012

The Honorable Bennie G. Thompson
Ranking Member
Committee on Homeland Security
House of Representatives

Dear Mr. Thompson:

Personnel security clearances allow government personnel to gain access to classified information that, through unauthorized disclosure, can in some cases cause exceptionally grave damage to U.S. national security. The September 11, 2001, attacks spurred an increase in the number of positions that require a security clearance across the executive branch. In tracking the number of people that have a security clearance, the Office of the Director of National Intelligence (ODNI) reported that as of October 1, 2011, over 4.8 million federal government civilian workforce, military personnel, and contractor employees held or were eligible to hold[1] a security clearance.[2, 3] This large number of personnel holding clearances coupled with risks to national security underscore the need for executive branch agencies to have a standard process to determine which positions require a security clearance. Additionally, a standard process is also needed to effectively manage costs, since agencies spend significant amounts annually on national security and other background investigations. For example, two of the agencies that grant the most security clearances, the Department of Defense (DOD) and the Department of Homeland Security (DHS) spent $787 million and at least

---

[1] In certain cases, individuals are investigated and deemed eligible to hold a security clearance. These individuals do not have access to classified information. However, access can be granted when the duties of their position require it.

[2] The ODNI report notes that there could be some duplicative entries. However, we did not verify the accuracy of this number.

[3] According to the Office of Personnel Management (OPM) fiscal year 2010 data, the federal government workforce consisted of over 4.4 million federal civilian employees and military personnel. This figure does not include contractors.

$57 million,[4] respectively, on suitability[5] and security clearance background investigations in fiscal year 2011.

In our previous work,[6] we identified the need for a sound requirements determination process to be considered in executive branch efforts to reform the security clearance process. Determining the requirements of a federal position includes assessing both the risk and sensitivity level associated with a position, which includes consideration of whether that position requires access to classified information. Specifically, we noted that the executive branch could address whether the numbers and levels of security clearances are appropriate and examine existing policies and practices to see if they need to be updated or otherwise modified. Developing a sound requirements process is important because requests for clearances for positions that do not need a clearance or need a lower level of clearance increase investigative workload and costs unnecessarily. For example, we reported in 2008 that changing the clearance needed for a position from secret to top secret increases the investigative workload for that one position about 20-fold. That is, top secret clearances must be performed twice as often as secret clearances (every 5 years versus 10 years) and require 10 times as many investigative staff hours (about 60 versus 6). More recently, our 2012 report found that the executive branch spent over $1 billion on background investigations for suitability and security clearances in fiscal year 2011.[7] Further, the Office of Personnel Management (OPM)—the federal investigative service provider for the majority of the executive branch—experienced an almost 79 percent increase in its reported costs

---

[4]For DHS, this $57 million represents only the amount that DHS paid OPM for suitability and security background investigations in 2010. In addition, DHS conducts some of its own background investigations.

[5]Determinations of suitability for government employment in positions in the competitive service, certain positions in the excepted service, and for career appointment in the Senior Executive Service include consideration of aspects of individuals' character or conduct that may have an impact on the integrity or efficiency of their service.

[6]GAO, *Personnel Clearances: Key Factors for Reforming the Security Clearance Process*, GAO-08-776T (Washington, D.C.: May 22, 2008) and *Personnel Clearances: Key Factors to Consider in Efforts to Reform Security Clearance Processes*, GAO-08-352T (Washington, D.C.: Feb. 27, 2008).

[7]GAO, *Background Investigations: Office of Personnel Management Needs to Improve Transparency of Its Pricing and Seek Cost Savings*, GAO-12-197 (Washington, D.C.: Feb. 28, 2012).

to conduct background investigations between fiscal years 2005 and 2011. Specifically, OPM's reported costs increased from about $602 million in fiscal year 2005 to almost $1.1 billion in fiscal year 2011 (in fiscal year 2011 dollars).

You asked us to evaluate federal government policies and practices for identifying positions that require security clearances, and analyze whether a uniform, consistent, and effective security clearance requirements determination process is in place. In response to this request, we examined the extent to which the executive branch has established (1) policies and procedures for agencies to use when first determining whether federal civilian positions require a security clearance and (2) policies and procedures for agencies to review and revise or validate existing federal civilian position security clearance requirements.

Specifically, the scope of our work focused on the security clearance requirements of federal civilian positions from selected components within DHS and DOD, due to the volume of clearances that these two agencies process. Within DHS, selected components included the U.S. Coast Guard, U.S. Immigration and Customs Enforcement, and the Transportation Security Administration. Within DOD, selected components included the headquarters-level elements of the Departments of the Army, the Navy, the Air Force, and Washington Headquarters Services, which provides human capital support for several nonservice DOD agencies and activities. For our first objective, to examine the extent to which the executive branch has established policies and procedures for agencies to use when first determining whether federal civilian positions require a security clearance, we interviewed key officials from the above-mentioned federal departments and selected components, as well as OPM and ODNI. In addition, we reviewed relevant Executive Orders including 10450, 12968, and 13467,[8]

---

[8]Executive Order No. 10450, *Security Requirements for Government Employment* (Apr. 27, 1953 as amended), Executive Order No. 12968, *Access to Classified Information* (Aug. 2, 1995 as amended), Executive Order No. 13467, *Reforming Processes Related to Suitability for Government Employment, Fitness for Contractor Employees, and Eligibility for Access to Classified National Security Information* (June 30, 2008).

Joint Reform Team[9] reports, and part 732 of Title 5 of the Code of Federal Regulations.[10] We also obtained and analyzed personnel security clearance policies within DHS, DOD, and the selected components within these departments. Further, we obtained and analyzed OPM's position designation tool because agencies we spoke with use the tool in the position designation process. For our second objective, to examine the extent to which the executive branch has policies and procedures for agencies to review and revise or validate existing federal civilian position security clearance requirements, we held meetings with knowledgeable officials from DHS, DOD, OPM, and ODNI. In addition, we reviewed part 732 of Title 5 of the Code of Federal Regulations. We also analyzed DHS's and DOD's personnel security policies, and the applicable policies of selected components within these departments. We conducted this performance audit from July 2011 through July 2012 in accordance with generally accepted government auditing standards. Those standards require that we plan and perform the audit to obtain sufficient, appropriate evidence to provide a reasonable basis for our findings and conclusions based on our audit objectives. We believe that the evidence obtained provides a reasonable basis for our findings and conclusions based on our objectives. A more thorough description of our scope and methodology is provided in appendix I.

Background

Security clearances are required for access to certain national security information, which is classified at one of three levels: top secret, secret, or confidential. The level of classification denotes the degree of protection required for information and the amount of damage that unauthorized disclosure could reasonably cause to national security.

---

[9]In 2007, DOD and ODNI formed the Joint Security and Suitability Reform Team, known as the Joint Reform Team, to execute joint reform efforts to achieve timeliness goals and improve the processes related to granting security clearances and determining suitability for government employment. Agencies included in this government-wide reform effort include the Office of Management and Budget, OPM, ODNI, and DOD's Under Secretary of Defense (Intelligence).

[10]Part 732 of Title 5 of the Code of Federal Regulations addresses national security positions within the federal government including the competitive service, the Senior Executive Service, and certain excepted service positions.

GAO-12-800 Security Clearances

Relevant Orders and Regulations

Executive Order 10450, which was originally issued in 1953, makes the heads of departments or agencies responsible for establishing and maintaining effective programs for ensuring that civilian employment and retention is clearly consistent with the interests of the national security. Agency heads are also responsible for designating positions within their respective agencies as sensitive if the occupant of that position could, by virtue of the nature of the position, bring about a material adverse effect on national security. In addition, Executive Order 12968, issued in 1995, is relevant to position designation because the order also makes the heads of agencies—including executive branch agencies and the military departments—responsible for establishing and maintaining an effective program to ensure that access to classified information by each employee is clearly consistent with the interests of national security. This order also states that, subject to certain exceptions, eligibility for access to classified information shall only be requested and granted on the basis of a demonstrated, foreseeable need for access. Further, part 732 of Title 5 of the Code of Federal Regulations provides requirements and procedures for the designation of national security positions,[11] which include positions that (1) involve activities of the government that are concerned with the protection of the nation from foreign aggression or espionage, and (2) require regular use of or access to classified national security information.

In addition, part 732 states that most federal government positions that could bring about, by virtue of the nature of the position, a material adverse effect on national security must be designated as a sensitive position and require a sensitivity level designation. The sensitivity level designation determines the type of background investigation required, with positions designated at a greater sensitivity level requiring a more extensive background investigation. Part 732 establishes three sensitivity levels—special-sensitive, critical-sensitive, and noncritical-sensitive—which are described in figure 1. According to OPM, positions that an agency designates as special-sensitive and critical-sensitive require a background investigation that typically results in a top secret clearance. Noncritical-sensitive positions typically require an investigation that supports a secret or confidential clearance. OPM also defines non-sensitive positions that do not have a national security element, but still

---

[11]Those requirements in Part 732 apply to national security positions in the competitive service, Senior Executive Service positions filled by career appointment within the executive branch, and certain excepted service positions.

require a designation of risk for suitability purposes. That risk level determines the type of investigation required for those positions. Those investigations include aspects of an individual's character or conduct that may have an effect on the integrity or efficiency of his or her service.

Position Designation Process

The personnel security clearance process begins when a human resources or security professional determines a position's level of sensitivity, which includes consideration of whether or not a position requires access to classified information and, if required, the level of access. DHS and DOD follow a general process for determining whether a federal civilian position requires access to classified information, which informs whether a position requires a security clearance. This process is described in figure 1 below and is based on our review of the corresponding guidance and testimonial evidence gathered during interviews with DHS and DOD officials. In addition, a more thorough description of DHS and DOD component-level policies appears in appendix II.

Figure 1: DHS and DOD Security Clearance Determination Process for Federal Civilian Positions

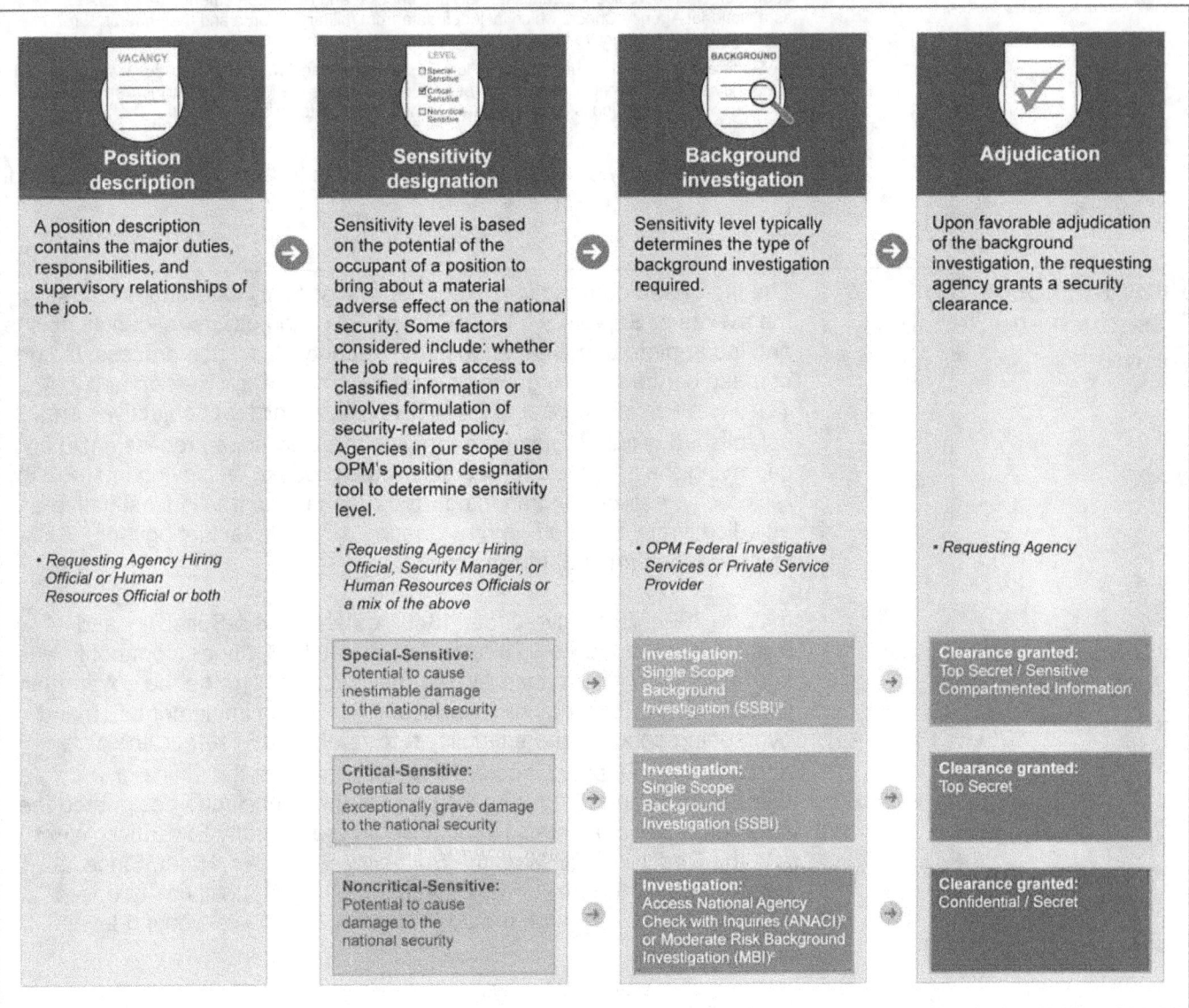

Source: GAO analysis of Department of Homeland Security (DHS) and Department of Defense (DOD) data.

[a]A Single Scope Background Investigation (SSBI) is conducted so that an individual can obtain a top secret clearance (including Sensitive Compartmented Information and Q access) and includes a review of the locations where an individual has lived, attended school, and worked. In addition, an SSBI includes interviews with four references who have social knowledge of the subject, interviews with former spouses, and a financial record check.

[b]An Access National Agency Check and Inquiries (ANACI) is used for the initial investigation for federal employees at the confidential and secret access levels. It consists of employment checks, education checks, residence checks, reference checks, and law enforcement agency checks, as well as a National Agency Check, which includes data from military records and the Federal Bureau of Investigation's investigative index.

[c]A Moderate Risk Background Investigation (MBI) includes an ANACI and provides issue-triggered enhanced subject interviews with issue resolution. DHS uses the MBI for non-critical sensitive positions when a position is first designated as high, moderate, or low risk.

The personnel security clearance process is further described in appendix III.

Personnel Security Clearance and Suitability Reforms

The increased demand for personnel with security clearances following the events of September 11, 2001, led GAO and others to identify delays and incomplete documentation in the security clearance process. In light of these concerns, Congress passed the Intelligence Reform and Terrorism Prevention Act of 2004 (IRTPA),[12] which set objectives and established requirements for improving the clearance process, including improving the timeliness of the clearance process, achieving interagency reciprocity, establishing an integrated database to track investigative and adjudicative information, and evaluating available technology for investigations and adjudications.

In June 2008, Executive Order 13467 established a Suitability and Security Clearance Performance Accountability Council, commonly known as the Performance Accountability Council, to be the government-wide governance structure responsible for driving implementation and overseeing security and suitability reform efforts.[13] Further, the order appointed the Deputy Director for Management at the Office of Management and Budget as the chair of the council and designated the Director of National Intelligence (DNI) as the Security Executive Agent and the Director of OPM as the Suitability Executive Agent. Since its establishment, the Performance Accountability Council has released several reports[14] through the Joint Reform Team—its working-level

---

[12]Pub. L. No. 108-458 (2004) (relevant sections codified at 50 U.S.C. § 435b).

[13]Executive Order 13467 calls for investigations of suitability and security to be aligned using consistent standards, to the extent practicable.

[14]Joint Security and Suitability Reform Team, *Security and Suitability Process Reform* (Washington, D.C.: April 2008 and updated December 2008); and Performance Accountability Council, *Security and Suitability Process Reform: Strategic Framework* (Washington, D.C.: February 2010).

predecessor that continues to focus on the reform effort—detailing reform-related plans, including a February 2010 strategic framework that established goals, performance measures, roles and responsibilities, and proposed metrics for determining the quality of security clearance investigations and adjudications. Those reports contained a reform plan that outlined a new seven-step process for end-to-end suitability and security clearance reform, see figure 2 below. According to ODNI officials, the first step—to "validate need,"—focuses on ensuring that the sensitivity level of positions is designated appropriately on the basis of mission needs, among other things.

Figure 2: Seven-Step Process for Suitability and Security Clearance Reform

Validate need	eApplication	Automated record checks (ARC)	eAdjudication	Enhanced subject interview	Expandable focused investigation	Continuous evaluation
Validate hiring and clearing request against mission needs	Interactive tool with branching questions to develop information on which to base evaluation	Utilize both government and commercial data for investigations at all tiers	Automated electronic clearance decision applying well-defined business rules to nonissue secret cases	In-depth subject interview based on application information and results of ARCs	Target use of human investigative resources to focus on issue resolution or mitigation	Utilize ARCs annually for all Top Secret / Sensitive Compartmented Information cleared personnel; no less than once every 5 years for those with Secret clearance

Source: GAO analysis of the Performance Accountability Council's *Security and Suitability Process Reform Strategic Framework,* February 2010.

Separate from, but related to, security clearances are determinations of suitability that the executive branch uses to ensure individuals are suitable, based on character and conduct, for federal employment in their agency or position.[15] Suitability requirements sometimes overlap with national security requirements. For example, the Department of Justice checks suitability to ensure that applicants for jobs with the Drug Enforcement Agency have never used illegal drugs. In addition, Health and Human Services checks the suitability of applicants for jobs working with children. Similarly, the Intelligence Community requires polygraph evaluations, among other things, to determine suitability for most intelligence positions. OPM was involved in many aspects of the suitability investigation process under Part 731 of Title 5 of the Code of

---

[15]See part 731of Title 5 of the Code of Federal Regulations.

GAO-12-800 Security Clearances

Federal Regulations, prior to the issuance of Executive Order 13467 and, as the Suitability Executive Agent, the Director continues to be responsible for developing and implementing uniform and consistent policies and procedures to ensure the effective, efficient, and timely completion of background investigations and adjudications relating to determinations of suitability.

In contrast, the DNI was assigned a new role. Executive Order 13467 states that the DNI, as the Security Executive Agent, is responsible for, among other things, developing uniform and consistent policies and procedures to ensure the effective, efficient, and timely completion of background investigations and adjudications relating to determinations of eligibility for access to classified information or eligibility to hold a sensitive position. In addition to these responsibilities, the Executive Order also provides the DNI the authority to issue guidelines and instructions to the heads of agencies to ensure appropriate uniformity, centralization, efficiency, effectiveness, and timeliness in processes relating to determinations by agencies of eligibility for access to classified information or eligibility to hold a sensitive position. The order also states that the Performance Accountability Council is responsible for ensuring that the Executive Agents align their respective processes. Finally, the order states that agency heads should implement any policy or procedure developed by either the Performance Accountability Council or Executive Agents under the order.

The Executive Branch Has Not Issued Clearly Defined Policy Guidance for Determining When a Federal Civilian Position Needs a Security Clearance

The DNI, in the capacity as Security Executive Agent responsible for developing uniform and consistent policies related to the security clearance process, has expressed intent to issue guidance relating to national security positions. However, the DNI has not provided agencies with clearly defined policy through regulation or other guidance to help ensure that executive branch agencies use appropriate and consistent criteria when determining if positions require a security clearance. Instead, executive branch agencies are using a position designation tool developed by OPM. This tool is designed to determine the sensitivity level of civilian positions which, in turn, informs the type of background investigation needed if a clearance is warranted. The DNI, however, did not have a role in its development even though the two Executive Agents are to align their respective processes. As a result, agency officials we met expressed mixed views on the effectiveness of the tool for national security positions.

The DNI Has a Role to Guide Agencies in Designating Positions for Security Clearances, But Has Not Provided Agencies with Clearly Defined Policy Guidance

According to Executive Order 13467, issued in June 2008, the DNI, as the Security Executive Agent, is responsible for developing uniform and consistent policies and procedures for determinations of eligibility for access to classified information or to hold a sensitive position. Further, the executive order states that agency heads shall assist the Performance Accountability Council and Executive Agents in carrying out any function under the order, which includes implementing any policies or procedures developed pursuant to the order. Although agency heads retain the flexibility to make determinations regarding which positions in their agency require a security clearance, the DNI is well positioned, by virtue of its role as the Security Executive Agent, to provide guidance to help align the process from agency to agency. The DNI, however, has not provided agencies with clearly defined policy or instructions.

OPM Has Developed a Tool to Help Agencies Determine the Proper Sensitivity Level for Most Federal Positions, but the Tool Lacks Input from the DNI

To assist with position designation, the Director of OPM—the Executive Agent for Suitability—has developed a process that includes a position designation system and corresponding automated tool to guide agencies in determining the proper sensitivity level for the majority of federal positions.[16] This tool—namely, the Position Designation of National Security and Public Trust Positions—enables a user to evaluate a position's national security and suitability requirements so as to determine a position's sensitivity and risk levels, which in turn dictate the type of background investigation that will be required for the individual who will occupy that position. In most agencies outside the Intelligence Community, OPM conducts the background investigations for both suitability and security clearance purposes. The tool does not directly determine whether a position requires a clearance, but rather helps determine the sensitivity level of the position. The determination to grant a clearance is based on whether a position requires access to classified information or other relevant factors, and, if access is required, the responsible official will designate the position to require a clearance.

---

[16]According to OPM's Federal Investigations Notice No. 10-06 *Position Designation Requirements* (Aug. 11, 2010), the tool is recommended for all agencies requesting OPM investigations and required for all positions in the competitive service, positions in the excepted service where the incumbent can be noncompetitively converted to the competitive service, and career appointments in the Senior Executive Service.

OPM developed the position designation system and automated tool for multiple reasons. First, OPM determined through a 2007 initiative[17] that its existing regulations and guidance for position designation were complex and difficult to apply, resulting in inconsistent designations. As a result of a recommendation from the initiative, OPM created a simplified position designation process in 2008. Additionally, OPM officials noted that the tool is to support the goals of the security and suitability reform efforts, which require proper designation of national security and suitability positions.

OPM first introduced the automated tool in November 2008, and issued an update of the tool in 2010. In August 2010, OPM issued guidance (1) recommending all agencies that request OPM background investigations use the tool and (2) requiring agencies to use the tool for all positions in the competitive service, positions in the excepted service where the incumbent can be noncompetitively converted to the competitive service, and career appointments in the Senior Executive Service. Both DHS and DOD components use the tool. A DHS instruction requires personnel to designate all DHS positions by using OPM's position sensitivity designation guidance, which is the basis of the tool.[18] In addition, DOD issued guidance in September 2011[19] requiring its personnel to use OPM's tool to determine the proper position sensitivity designation for new or vacant positions, including the establishment and reclassification of positions. ODNI officials told us that they believe OPM's tool is useful for determining a position's sensitivity level. However, despite the DNI's responsibility for policy related to ensuring uniformity in the security clearance process, ODNI officials noted that the DNI did not have input into recent revisions of OPM's position designation tool.

This lack of coordination for revising the tool exists, in part, because the execution of the roles and relationships between the Director of OPM and

---

[17]The Hadley-Springer commission was an initiative between OPM and the Assistant to the President for National Security Affairs that focused on simplifying the federal government investigative and adjudicative procedures to improve security requirements to determine eligibility for access to classified information, among other things.

[18]DHS Management Instruction 121-01-007, *Department of Homeland Security Personnel Suitability and Security Program* (June 2009).

[19]DOD Washington Headquarters Services, *Implementation of the Position Designation Automated Tool*, (Sept. 27, 2011).

GAO-12-800 Security Clearances

the DNI as Executive Agents are still evolving, although Executive Order 13467 defines responsibilities for each Executive Agent. Accordingly, we found that the Director of OPM and the DNI have not fully collaborated in executing their respective roles in the process for determining position designations. For example, OPM has had long-standing responsibility for establishing standards with respect to suitability for most federal government positions. Accordingly, the sections of the tool to be used for evaluating a position's suitability risk level are significantly more detailed than the sections designed to aid in designating the national security sensitivity level of the position. While most of OPM's position designation system, which is the basis of the tool, is devoted to suitability issues, only two pages are devoted to national security issues, despite the reference to national security in its title. Moreover, OPM did not seek to collaborate with the DNI when updating the tool in 2010. Similarly, in 2010, OPM initiated revisions to the part of the Code of Federal Regulations that pertain to national security positions.[20] According to OPM and ODNI officials, the revision is expected to clarify the standards for designating whether federal positions are national security sensitive, which will help agencies more accurately assess the sensitivity of a position. The sensitivity level includes consideration of whether a position is eligible for access to classified information and the level of access. Further, the revision is currently expected to update the definition of national security positions to include positions that could have a material impact on national security, but might not clearly fall within the current definition in part 732 of Title 5 of the Code of Federal Regulations. For example, such positions include those with duties that involve the protection of borders, ports, and critical infrastructure, as well as those with responsibilities related to public safety, law enforcement, and the protection of government information systems.

During our review, human capital and security officials from DHS and DOD and the selected components affirmed that they were using the existing tool to determine the sensitivity level required by a position. However, in the absence of clearly defined policy from the DNI and the lack of collaborative input into the tool's design, officials explained that they sometimes had difficulty in using the tool to designate the sensitivity level of national security positions.

---

[20]See 75 Federal Register 77783 (Dec. 14, 2010). The comment period for that draft revision ended on February 14, 2011. No final or interim rule has been issued, and no executive branch agency is currently subject to the proposed revision.

GAO-12-800 Security Clearances

Audits Show Problems with Position Designations

OPM regularly conducts audits of its executive branch customer agency personnel security and suitability programs, which include a review of position designation to assess the agencies' alignment with OPM's position designation guidance. In the audit reports we obtained, OPM found examples of inconsistency between agency position designation and OPM guidance, both before and after the implementation of OPM's tool. For instance, prior to the implementation of the tool, in a 2006 audit of an executive branch agency, OPM found that its sensitivity designations differed from the agency's designation in 13 of 23 positions. Specifically, OPM concluded that 11 positions were underdesignated, 1 position was overdesignated, and 1 position was adjusted. More recently, after the implementation of the tool, in an April 2012 audit of a DOD agency, OPM assessed the sensitivity levels of 39 positions, and OPM's designations differed from the agency's designations in 26 of those positions. In the April 2012 report, the DOD agency agreed with OPM's recommendations related to position designation, and the audit report confirmed that the agency had submitted evidence of corrective action in response to the position designation recommendations. OPM provided us with the results of 10 audits that it had conducted between 2005 and 2012, and 9 of those audit reports reflected inconsistencies between OPM position designation guidance and determinations of position sensitivity conducted by the agency. OPM officials noted, however, that they do not have the authority to direct agencies to make different designations because Executive Order 10450 provides agency heads with the ultimate responsibility for designating which positions are sensitive positions.

As of May 2012, the Naval Audit Service is currently finalizing its own internal audit on its top secret requirements determination process for civilian positions. While the results were not complete at the time of our review, officials explained to us that they began this audit to validate their top secret requirements and ensure that they have effective internal controls over their designation process.[21]

Agency Officials Had Mixed Views of Designation Tool

DHS and DOD officials expressed varying opinions regarding the tool. For instance, some of the officials we met raised concerns regarding the

---

[21]ODNI conducted a separate position designation audit in response to the Intelligence Authorization Act for Fiscal Year 2010, Pub. L. No. 111-259 (2010). In that report, ODNI found that the processes the executive branch agencies followed differed somewhat depending whether the position was civilian, military, or contractor.

guidance provided through the tool and expressed that they had difficulty implementing it. Specifically, officials from DHS's U.S. Immigration and Customs Enforcement stated that the use of the tool occasionally resulted in inconsistency, such as over- or underdesignating a position, and expressed a need for additional clear, easily interpreted guidance on designating national security positions. DOD officials stated that they have had difficulty implementing the tool because it focuses more on suitability than security, and the national security aspects of DOD's positions are of more concern to them than the suitability aspects. Further, an official from DOD's Office of the Under Secretary of Defense for Personnel and Readiness stated that the tool and DOD policy do not always align and that the tool does not cover the requirements for some DOD positions. For example, DOD's implementing guidance on using the tool states that terms differ between DOD's personnel security policy and the tool, and the tool might suggest different position sensitivity levels than DOD policy requires. Also, officials from the Air Force Personnel Security Office told us that they had challenges using the tool to classify civilian positions, including difficulty in linking the tool with Air Force practices for position designation. Moreover, an Air Force official stated a concern that the definition for national security positions is broadly written and could be considered to include all federal positions. Further, individuals responsible for making position designation determinations can easily reach different conclusions. For instance, officials from DHS's U.S. Immigration and Customs Enforcement stated that the tool is not necessarily intuitive and users of the tool need to understand its nuances in order to avoid overdesignating a position. Conversely, officials from the U.S. Coast Guard stated that they found the tool to be intuitive, and that it helps to ensure consistency in designation. Finally, officials from the Transportation Security Administration noted that the tool is user friendly and provides consistency for managers.

Recently, we have seen indications that the Executive Agents are working to align their respective processes. According to OPM's website, OPM has conferred with the Office of Management and Budget (OMB) concerning the possibility of reissuing pertinent sections of the Code of Federal Regulations jointly with ODNI, with a targeted issuance before the end of the 2012 calendar year. ODNI officials also stated their intention to work with OPM on the revision effort. ODNI officials further acknowledged that they are collaborating with OPM to reach agreement on their respective roles as Executive Agents. Our prior work has found that two or more agencies with related goals can benefit from enhancing their collaboration in various areas to achieve common outcomes.[22]

The Executive Branch Does Not Have a Consistent Process for Reviewing and Validating Existing Security Clearance Requirements for Civilian Positions

According to Executive Order 12968, the number of employees that each agency determines is eligible for access to classified information shall be kept to the minimum required, and, subject to certain exceptions, eligibility shall be requested or granted only on the basis of a demonstrated, foreseeable need for access. Additionally, Executive Order 12968 states that access to classified information shall be terminated when an employee no longer has a need for access, and that requesting or approving eligibility for access in excess of the actual requirements is prohibited. Also, Executive Order 13467 authorizes the DNI to issue guidelines or instructions to the heads of agencies regarding, among other things, uniformity in determining eligibility for access to classified information. However, the DNI has not issued policies and procedures for agencies to review and revise or validate the existing clearance requirements for their federal civilian positions to ensure that clearances are kept to a minimum and reserved only for those positions with security clearance requirements that are in accordance with the national security needs of the time.

As previously noted, OPM published a December 2010 notice in the Federal Register of a proposed revision to the Code of Federal Regulations to clarify the policy for designating national security positions. Again, as we previously noted, OPM's website states that OPM has conferred with OMB concerning the possibility of reissuing pertinent sections of the Code of Federal Regulations jointly with ODNI. One feature of the proposed revision would require all federal agencies to conduct a onetime review of position descriptions and requirements over a period of 2 years to ensure that all positions are properly designated using the revision's updated definition for national security positions. Position descriptions not only identify the major duties and responsibilities of the position, but they also play a critical role in recruitment, training,

---

[22]GAO, *Results-Oriented Government: Practices That Can Help Enhance and Sustain Collaboration among Federal Agencies*, GAO-06-15 (Washington, D.C.: Oct. 21, 2005). The areas for agencies to enhance collaboration include defining a common outcome; establishing joint strategies to achieve the outcome; agreeing upon agency roles and responsibilities; establishing compatible policies, procedures, and other means to operate across agency boundaries; and developing mechanisms to monitor, evaluate, and report the results of collaborative efforts.

and performance management, among other things. While position descriptions may change, so can the national security environment as previously observed.

During our review of several DHS and DOD components, we found that officials were aware of the need to keep the number of security clearances to a minimum but were not always subject to a requirement to review and validate the security clearance needs of existing positions on a periodic basis. We found, instead, that agencies' policies provide for a variety of practices for reviewing the clearance needs of federal civilian positions. According to DHS guidance, supervisors are responsible for ensuring that (1) position designations are updated when a position undergoes major changes (e.g., changes in missions and functions, job responsibilities, work assignments, legislation, or classification standards), and (2) position security designations are assigned as new positions are created. Some components have additional requirements to review position designation more regularly to cover positions other than those newly created or vacant. For example,

- U.S. Coast Guard guidance[23] states that hiring officials and supervisors should review position descriptions even when there is no vacancy and, as appropriate, either revise or review them.
- According to officials in U.S. Immigration and Customs Enforcement, supervisors are supposed to review position descriptions annually during the performance review process to ensure that the duties and responsibilities on the position description are up-to-date and accurate. However, officials stated that U.S. Immigration and Customs Enforcement does not have policies or requirements in place to ensure any particular level of detail in that review.

DOD's personnel security regulation and other guidance[24] provides DOD components with criteria to consider when determining whether a position is sensitive or requires access to classified information, and some of the components also have developed their own guidance.

---

[23]U.S. Coast Guard, CG-121, *Civilian Hiring Guide for Supervisors and Managers*, ver. 2 (June 11, 2010).

[24]DOD 5200.2-R, *Department of Defense Personnel Security Program* (January 1987, reissued incorporating changes Feb. 23, 1996) as modified by Under Secretary of Defense Memorandum, *Implementation of the Position Designation Automated Tool* (May 10, 2011).

- An Air Force Instruction requires commanders to review all military and civilian position designations annually to ensure proper level of access to classified information.[25]
- The Army issued a memorandum in 2006 that required an immediate review of position sensitivity designations for all Army civilian positions by the end of the calendar year and requires subsequent reviews biennially.[26] That memorandum further states that if a review warrants a change in position sensitivity affecting an individual's access to classified information, then access should be administratively adjusted and the periodic reinvestigation submitted accordingly. However, officials explained that improper position sensitivity designations continue to occur in the Army because they have a limited number of personnel in the security office relative to workload, and they only spot check clearance requests to ensure that they match the level of clearance required.
- Officials from DOD's Washington Headquarters Services told us that they have an informal practice of reviewing position descriptions and security designations for vacant or new positions, but they do not have a schedule for conducting periodic reviews of personnel security designations for already-filled positions.

These various policies notwithstanding, agency officials told us that they are implemented inconsistently.

Some of the components we met were in the process of conducting a onetime review of position designation during our review. For example, Transportation Security Administration officials stated that they reevaluated all of their position descriptions over the last 2 years because the agency determined that the re-evaluation of its position designations would improve operational efficiency by ensuring that positions were appropriately designated by using OPM's updated position designation tool. Further, those officials told us that they review position descriptions as positions become vacant or are created. Between fiscal years 2010 and 2011, while the Transportation Security Administration's overall workforce increased from 61,586 to 66,023, the number of investigations for top secret clearances decreased from 1,483 to 1,127. In March 2011, the Naval Audit Service begin an audit of its top secret requirements

---

[25] Air Force Instruction 31-501, *Personnel Security Program Management* (Jan. 27, 2005).

[26] Army Director of Counterintelligence, Human Intelligence, Disclosure and Security Memorandum, *Civilian Position Sensitivity Review* (Dec. 31, 2006).

determination process for civilian positions at selected activities to verify that civilian top secret clearances are based on valid requirements and that effective internal controls over the top secret requirements determination process are in place. According to a Navy official, the results of the audit were still undergoing the Navy's internal review process as of May 2012.

There is a cost to conducting background investigations, and a potential for dollar savings when overdesignated positions are identified. DHS and DOD officials acknowledged to us that overdesignating a position can result in expenses for unnecessary investigations. When a position is overdesignated, additional resources are unnecessarily spent conducting the investigation and adjudication of a background investigation that exceeds agency requirements. As stated earlier in this report, the investigative workload for a top secret clearance is about 20-times greater than that of a secret clearance because it must be periodically reinvestigated twice as often as secret clearance investigations (every 5 years versus every 10 years) and requires 10 times as many investigative staff hours. The fiscal year 2012 base price for a top secret clearance investigation conducted by OPM is $4,005 and the periodic reinvestigation is $2,711, while the base price of an investigation for a secret clearance is $260. Further, the base price of a Moderate Risk Background Investigation—most commonly used by DHS, according to officials—is $752. However, we did not find policies in which position designation reviews were linked to the position holders' periodic reinvestigations. In contrast, underdesignating a position carries security risks, such as the potential release of classified information or the placement of a person in a position for which they have not been properly cleared.

Agencies employ varying practices because the DNI has not established a requirement that executive branch agencies consistently review and revise or validate existing position designations on a recurring basis. Such a recurring basis could include reviewing position designations during the periodic reinvestigation process. Without a requirement to consistently review, revise, or validate existing security clearance position designations, executive branch agencies—such as DHS and DOD—may be hiring and budgeting for both initial and periodic security clearance investigations using position descriptions and security clearance requirements that no longer reflect national security needs. Finally, since reviews are not being done consistently, DHS and DOD and other executive branch agencies cannot have reasonable assurances that they are keeping to a minimum the number of positions that require security clearances on the basis of a demonstrated and foreseeable need for access.

Conclusions

Executive Order 13467, issued in June 2008, established a Suitability and Security Clearance Performance Accountability Council and appointed the DNI as the Security Executive Agent and the Director of OPM as the Suitability Executive Agent. However, while the order gives the Executive Agents the authority to issue policy, the DNI has not provided executive branch agencies with clearly defined policy and procedures for determining whether federal civilian positions require a security clearance. Until the DNI articulates such policy and procedures, executive branch agencies, such as DHS and DOD, will not have a foundation on which to build consistent and uniform policies. Further, Executive Order 13467 indicates that executive branch policies and procedures relating to, among other things, suitability and eligibility for access to classified information shall be aligned using consistent standards to the extent possible. However, OPM updated its position designation tool in 2010 without input from the DNI. Without collaborative input from both OPM and DNI in future revisions to the tool, executive branch agencies will continue to risk making security clearance determinations that are inconsistent or at improper levels. Finally, while Executive Order 12968 says that clearances should, subject to certain exceptions, be granted only on the basis of a demonstrated need for access and kept to a minimum, the DNI has not issued guidance that requires agencies to review and revise or validate their existing federal civilian position designations. Until the DNI does so, DHS and DOD, along with other executive branch agencies, cannot have reasonable assurances that all security clearance designations are correct, which could compromise national security if positions are underdesignated, or create unnecessary and costly investigative coverage if positions are overdesignated.

Recommendations for Executive Action

We recommend that the DNI, in coordination with the Director of OPM and other executive branch agencies as appropriate, issue clearly defined policy and procedures for federal agencies to follow when determining if federal civilian positions require a security clearance.

In addition, we recommend that, once the policy and procedures are issued, the DNI and the Director of OPM collaborate in their respective roles as Executive Agents to revise the position designation tool to reflect that guidance.

Finally, we recommend that the DNI, in coordination with the Director of OPM and other executive branch agencies as appropriate, issue guidance to require executive branch agencies to periodically review and revise or validate the designation of all federal civilian positions.

Agency Comments and Our Evaluation

We provided a draft of this report to ODNI, OPM, DHS, and DOD for comment. Written comments from ODNI, OPM, and DHS are reprinted in their entirety in appendices IV, V, and VI respectively. Technical comments were provided separately by ODNI, OPM, and DHS, and were incorporated as appropriate. DOD concurred with the report without written comment. We also provided a draft of the report to OMB for information purposes.

ODNI Comments

In commenting on this report, ODNI stated that the report is a fair assessment of existing executive branch policies for determining security clearance requirements for federal civilian positions. The DNI has a lead or collaborative role in our recommendations, and ODNI concurred with all three. First, ODNI concurred with our recommendation that the DNI, in coordination with the Director of OPM and other executive branch agencies as appropriate, issue clearly defined policy and procedures for federal agencies to follow when determining if federal civilian positions require a security clearance. ODNI agreed that executive branch agencies require simplified and uniform policy guidance to assist in determining appropriate sensitivity designations, and cited steps it is taking in coordination with OPM, DOD, and OMB. Specifically, ODNI acknowledged its work with OMB and OPM to jointly issue revisions to part 732 of Title 5 of the Code of Federal Regulations by the end of 2012. Second, ODNI concurred with our recommendation that, once the policy and procedures are issued, the DNI coordinate with the Director of OPM to revise the position designation tool to reflect that guidance. ODNI stated that it plans to work with OPM and other executive branch agencies through the Security Executive Agent Advisory Committee to develop a position designation tool that provides detailed descriptions of the types of positions where the occupant could bring about a material adverse impact to national security due to the duties and responsibilities of the position. ODNI stated its belief that a tool that provides agencies with detailed descriptions of this type will bring about greater uniformity across the government in agency position designations. Third, ODNI concurred with our recommendation that the DNI, in coordination with the Director of OPM and other executive branch agencies as appropriate, issue guidance to require executive branch agencies to periodically review and revise or validate the designation of all federal civilian positions. ODNI agreed with our assessment that the duties and responsibilities of federal positions may be subject to change, and stated that it plans to work with OPM and other executive branch agencies through the Security Executive Agent Advisory Committee to ensure that position designation policies and procedures include a provision for periodic reviews.

While ODNI recognized that the emphasis of this report is on civilian positions that require access to classified information, it wished to emphasize that the DNI's role as Security Executive Agent under Executive Order 13467 applies to all sensitive positions, and that positions that require access to classified information are a subset of all sensitive positions. ODNI stated that any guidance issued by the Security Executive Agent will cover all sensitive positions and associated investigative standards and adjudicative guidelines.

OPM Comments

OPM also commented on all three of the recommendations in this report in its written comments. OPM concurred with our second recommendation, which is addressed more directly to OPM, that its Director collaborate with the DNI in their respective roles as executive agents to revise the position designation tool to reflect updated federal position designation guidance. OPM stated that it committed to doing so in a February 2010 strategic framework document which was executed by officials within OMB, OPM, DOD, and ODNI. OPM also acknowledged that any revisions to the tool need to await final action with respect to proposed position designation regulations, which is consistent with our recommendation. In addition, OPM summarized executive orders that describe its authority. OPM also supported our third recommendation that the DNI, in coordination with the Director of OPM and other executive branch agencies as appropriate, issue guidance to require executive branch agencies to periodically review and revise or validate the designation of all federal civilian positions. OPM stated that it would be pleased to work with the DNI on guidance concerning periodic reviews of existing designations.

While ODNI concurred with our first recommendation—that the DNI, in coordination with the Director of OPM and other executive branch agencies as appropriate, issue clearly defined policy and procedures for federal agencies to follow when determining whether federal civilian positions require a security clearance—OPM stated that it is not clear to OPM that it has a significant role in prescribing the policy and procedures for federal agencies to follow when determining if a federal civilian position requires a security clearance. The basis for OPM's statement is Executive Order 12968 (as amended by Executive Order 13467), which gives agency heads the ultimate responsibility to grant or deny security clearances, subject to investigative standards and adjudicative guidelines prescribed by the DNI. In this report, we acknowledge that authority to grant or deny a security clearance resides with agency heads under Executive Order 12968. However, as we also state in our report, Executive Order 13467 provides the DNI the authority to issue guidelines and instructions to the heads of agencies to ensure appropriate uniformity, centralization, efficiency, effectiveness, and timeliness in processes relating to determinations by agencies of eligibility for access to classified information or eligibility to hold a sensitive position. Further, as we state in our report, this Executive Order established a Suitability and Security Clearance Performance Accountability Council to be the government-wide governance structure responsible for driving implementation and overseeing security and suitability reform efforts. This order appointed the DNI as the Security Executive Agent and the Director of OPM as the Suitability Executive Agent, and calls for investigations of suitability and security to be aligned using consistent standards, to the extent practicable. Therefore, we continue to believe that additional guidance from the Security Executive Agent—the DNI—would help align processes across multiple executive branch agencies, and note that ODNI agreed with this assessment. Further, we included OPM in our recommendation as a consulting agency in its role as the Suitability Executive Agent and because, according to OPM, it is the investigative service provider for much of the executive branch. Finally, we recommended that the DNI work with other agencies as necessary in an acknowledgement of the joint nature of reform effort and its oversight structure through the Performance Accountability Council.

OPM's response to this report discussed other points for consideration, which are summarized below.

Relationship between the existing position designation tool and security clearances: OPM stated in its comments that one of the premises upon which this report is based is not accurate. Specifically, OPM asserted that we repeatedly posited that agencies must perform the national security designation in order to know whether the occupant will require a security clearance when, in fact, whether the occupant of a particular position will need access to classified information or eligibility for such access (i.e. a security clearance) is one of the factors that help determine whether a position is sensitive. Accordingly, OPM wrote that there is no basis for

GAO to conclude that OPM's position designation tool affects how agencies determine whether the occupant of a position requires access to classified information or eligibility for such access. We state in our report that to assist with position designation, the Director of OPM has developed a process that includes a position designation system and corresponding tool. We continue by stating that the tool does not directly determine whether a position requires a clearance, but rather helps determine the sensitivity of the position, which informs the type of investigation needed. We believe that these statements are consistent with OPM's explanations and, therefore, do not believe that one of the premises upon which this report is based is inaccurate. However, we have reviewed and made revisions to other statements in our final report to ensure consistency with this point.

Additional need for guidance to support the position designation tool: OPM noted that it provided us with copies of audits that OPM had performed on agencies that employ competitive service civilian personnel, where it observed inconsistencies in agency application of the tool. In its comments, OPM cited several reasons why this might happen. We believe this is consistent with our findings that OPM found examples of inconsistency between agency position designation and OPM guidance, and also that officials from executive branch departments expressed varying opinions to us regarding the tool. In response to other discussion in our report about the tool, OPM stated that its proposed revision to part 732 of Title 5 of the Code of Federal Regulations was intended to establish a basis for more detailed guidance. We also note, as previously discussed, that OPM concurred with our recommendation to collaborate with the DNI to revise the tool.

DHS Comments

In its written comments, DHS noted GAO's positive acknowledgement of DHS' efforts to ensure that only those who need a security clearance are authorized one. Although the report does not contain any recommendations specifically directed to DHS, the Department stated that it remains committed to being an active member of the government-wide Suitability and Security Clearance Performance Accountability Council.

We are sending copies of this report to the House Committee on Homeland Security. We are also sending copies to the Director of National Intelligence, the Director of the Office of Personnel Management, the Secretary of Homeland Security, the Secretary of Defense, and the

Office of Management and Budget. This report will also be available at no charge on the GAO website at http://www.gao.gov.

If you or your staff have any questions about this report, please contact me at (202) 512-3604 or farrellb@gao.gov. Contact points for our Offices of Congressional Relations and Public Affairs may be found on the last page of this report. GAO staff who made major contributions to this report are listed in appendix VII.

Sincerely yours,

Brenda S. Farrell
Director, Defense Capabilities and Management

Appendix I: Scope and Methodology

This report reviewed government policies and practices for identifying federal civilian positions that require security clearances, and analyzed whether a uniform, consistent, and effective security clearance requirements determination process is in place. Our work focused on the Office of the Director of National Intelligence (ODNI), on the basis of its role to develop personnel security clearance policy and guidance for the federal government. Further, the scope of our work focused more specifically on the security clearance requirements of federal civilian positions from selected components within the Department of Homeland Security (DHS) and the Department of Defense (DOD), because of the volume of clearances that these two agencies process. Within DHS, selected components include the U.S. Coast Guard, U.S. Immigration and Customs Enforcement, and the Transportation Security Administration. Within DOD, selected components include the headquarters level elements of the Departments of the Army, the Navy, the Air Force, and the Washington Headquarters Services. We also included the Office of Personnel Management (OPM) in our review on the basis of its role implementing security clearance reform and as the primary investigative service provider of the federal government. See table 1 for a complete list of the agencies and departments interviewed for our review.

Table 1: Executive Branch Agencies and Offices Interviewed

Executive branch agency	Associated departments and offices
Department of Homeland Security (DHS)	• Office of the Chief Human Capital Officer
	• Office of the Chief Security Officer
	• U.S. Coast Guard
	• U.S. Immigration and Customs Enforcement
	• Transportation Security Administration
Department of Defense (DOD)	• Office of the Undersecretary of Defense for Intelligence
	• Office of the Undersecretary of Defense for Personnel and Readiness
	• Army's Office of the Deputy Chief of Staff (G-2)
	• Army's Personnel Security Organization (G-3/5/7)
	• Army's Human Resources Program Development Division
	• Air Force's Manpower Agency and Central Civilian Classification Office
	• Air Force's Personnel Security Office
	• Head of Security Policy (Personnel, Information, and Industrial) for the Navy
	• Navy Office of Civilian Human Resources
	• Washington Headquarters Services
	• Defense Manpower and Data Center
Office of Personnel Management (OPM)	• Federal Investigative Services
Office of the Director of National Intelligence(ODNI)	• Joint Reform Team representatives

Source: GAO.

To determine the extent to which the executive branch has established policies and procedures for agencies to use when first determining whether federal civilian positions require a security clearance, we interviewed key federal officials from the above mentioned federal agencies and selected components, as well as OPM and ODNI. We reviewed relevant Executive Orders including 10450, 12968, and 13467,[1] Joint Reform Team[2] reports, OPM and ODNI audits, and part 732 of Title 5 of the Code of Federal Regulations[3]. We also reviewed OPM's proposed revision to the Code of Federal Regulations, which aims to clarify the policy for designating national security positions that was published in the Federal Register in December 2010. We obtained and analyzed personnel security clearance policies within DHS, DOD, and the selected components within these departments to identify the extent to which they have outlined processes for individuals responsible for determining if federal civilian positions require a security clearance. In addition, we obtained and analyzed OPM's position designation system and tool because agencies we visited use the tool in the position designation process.

To determine the extent to which the executive branch has established policies and procedures for agencies to review and revise or validate existing federal civilian position security clearance requirements, we interviewed knowledgeable officials from the federal agencies and selected components in table 1. We reviewed part 732 of Title 5 of the Code of Federal Regulations to identify the extent to which it delineates processes and responsibilities for federal agencies to review and revise or validate whether federal civilian positions require a security clearance. We also analyzed DHS's and DOD's personnel security policies, and the applicable policies of selected components within these departments to identify the extent to which each department and selected component has

---

[1]Executive Order No. 10450, *Security Requirements for Government Employment* (Apr. 27, 1953 as amended), Executive Order No. 12968, *Access to Classified Information* (Aug. 2, 1995 as amended), Executive Order No. 13467, *Reforming Processes Related to Suitability for Government Employment, Fitness for Contractor Employees, and Eligibility for Access to Classified National Security Information* (June 30, 2008).

[2]In 2007, DOD and the Office of the Director of National Intelligence formed the Joint Security Clearance Process Reform Team, known as the Joint Reform Team, to execute joint reform efforts to achieve timeliness goals and improve the processes related to granting security clearances and determining suitability for government employment. Agencies included in this government-wide reform effort include the Office of Management and Budget, OPM, ODNI, and DOD's Office of the Undersecretary of Defense for Intelligence.

[3]5 C.F.R. part 732 addresses national security positions within the federal government including the competitive service, the Senior Executive Service, and certain excepted service positions.

established processes for reviewing, revising, and validating existing federal civilian position security clearance requirements.

We conducted this performance audit from July 2011 through July 2012 in accordance with generally accepted government auditing standards. Those standards require that we plan and perform the audit to obtain sufficient, appropriate evidence to provide a reasonable basis for our findings and conclusions based on our audit objectives. We believe that the evidence obtained provides a reasonable basis for our findings and conclusions based on our objectives.

Appendix II: Position Designation Guidance

The Department of Homeland Security (DHS), the Department of Defense (DOD), and their respective components have developed policies and procedures that relate to position designation. Both DHS and DOD policies provide criteria, in addition to those outlined in the Office of Personnel Management's (OPM) tool, for position designating officials to use in determining the sensitivity level of the position. Table 2 below provides a descriptive comparison of DHS- and DOD-specific position designation guidance.

Table 2: Summary of Selected DHS and DOD Position Designation Guidance

Clearance level	Sensitivity level	DHS criteria	DOD criteria
Top Secret / Sensitive Compartmented Information	Special-Sensitive (positions with the potential to cause inestimable damage to the national security)	Any position designated at a level higher than Critical-Sensitive by a document that complements Executive Order 10450 and Executive Order 12968.	Positions that require access to Sensitive Compartmented Information (SCI). Positions that require access to unique or uniquely productive intelligence sources or methods vital to the United States security. Positions that could cause inestimable damage and/or compromise technologies, plans, or procedures vital to the strategic advantage of the United States. Any other positions designated by appropriate officials.
Top Secret	Critical-Sensitive (positions with the potential to cause exceptionally grave damage to the national security)	Positions that have the potential to cause exceptionally grave damage to the national security. These positions may include access up to, and including, Top Secret national security information or materials; or other positions related to national security, regardless of duties, that require the same degree of trust.	Access to Top Secret information. Development or approval of plans, policies, or programs that affect the overall operations of DOD or DOD component. Development or approval of war plans. Investigative and certain investigative support duties, the issuance of personnel security clearances or the making of personnel security determinations. Fiduciary, public contact, or other duties. Duties falling under Special Access programs. Category I automated data processing positions responsible for, among other things, the development and administration of agency computer security programs. Any other position so designated by the Head of the DOD component or designee.

Clearance level	Sensitivity level	DHS criteria	DOD criteria
Secret or Confidential	Noncritical-Sensitive (positions with the potential to cause serious damage to the national security)	Positions that have the potential to cause serious damage to the national security. These positions involve either access to Secret or Confidential national security information materials, or duties that may adversely affect, directly or indirectly, the national security operations of the Department.	Access to Secret or Confidential information. Security police / provost marshal-type duties involving the enforcement of law and security duties involving the protection and safeguarding of DOD personnel and property. Category II automated data processing positions responsible for, among other things, systems design, operation, testing, maintenance, and monitoring under technical review of Category I automated data processing positions. Duties involving education and orientation of DOD personnel. Duties involving the design, operation, or maintenance of intrusion detection systems deployed to safeguard DOD personnel and property. Any other position so designated by the Head of the DOD component or designee.

Source: DHS and DOD.

Note: Data are from DHS, Management Instruction 121-01-007, The Department of Homeland Security Personnel Suitability and Security Program (June 2009), and DOD, Enclosure to the Under Secretary of Defense for Personnel and Readiness Memorandum, *Implementation of the Position Designation Automated Tool* (May 10, 2011).

Department of Homeland Security

DHS's management instruction regarding the personnel security and suitability program (DHS Management Instruction 121-01-007) defines sensitivity levels and instructs the DHS components to follow OPM's position sensitivity designation guidance when determining the proper sensitivity level for civilian positions. Further, the supervising official with sufficient knowledge of duty assignments is responsible for collaborating with Human Resources and assigning position sensitivity designations and then those designations are subject to final approval by the component's respective Personnel Security Office.

Immigration and Customs Enforcement: In addition to DHS's management directive, Immigration and Customs Enforcement officials confirmed that they are using OPM's position sensitivity designation guidance and position designation tool to ensure that their civilian positions have the proper sensitivity level. According to these officials, the Immigration and Customs Enforcement's Office of Professional Responsibility and Office of Human Capital work with the program offices to establish and validate position security designations.

Transportation Security Administration: In addition to DHS's management directive, the Transportation Security Administration developed informal guidance on the position designation process and uses OPM's position designation tool to determine the sensitivity level for its positions. The Transportation Security Administration Personnel Security Section requires the manager to confirm that access to classified information is required to perform the duties of the position. In addition, the Transportation Security Administration's Personnel Security Section does a final review of all position and risk designations.

U.S. Coast Guard: According to U.S. Coast Guard officials, the U.S. Coast Guard follows the criteria for position designation laid out in the Commandant of the Coast Guard Instruction 5520.12C, *Personnel Security and Suitability Program*. In addition, those officials indicated that the U.S. Coast Guard uses OPM's position designation tool for determining the sensitivity level for civilian positions. As part of a standard hiring practice, supervisors engage Human Resources with a request for personnel action. This initiates the prerecruitment phase of the process where the need of the position is validated, the position description is reviewed and updated, the job analysis is confirmed, and the recruitment strategy is executed.

Department of Defense

DOD's personnel security regulation and other guidance[1] provide the DOD components with detailed criteria to consider when determining whether a position requires access to classified information. Although DOD's policy is also under revision, the current policy incorporates OPM's definitions for critical-sensitive and noncritical sensitive positions. Further, DOD's regulation specifically states that personnel security clearances shall not normally be issued:

- to persons in nonsensitive positions;
- to persons whose regular duties do not require authorized access to classified information;
- for ease of movement of persons within a restricted area whose duties do not require access to classified information;

---

[1]DOD 5200.2-R, *Department of Defense Personnel Security Program* (January 1987, reissued incorporating changes Feb. 23, 1996) as modified by Under Secretary of Defense for Personnel and Readiness Memorandum, *Implementation of the Position Designation Automated Tool* (May 10, 2011).

- to persons who may only have inadvertent access to sensitive information or areas, such as guards, emergency service personnel, firefighters, doctors, nurses, police, ambulance drivers, or similar personnel;
- to persons working in shipyards whose duties do not require access to classified information;
- to persons who can be prevented from accessing classified information by being escorted by cleared personnel;
- to food service personnel, vendors and similar commercial sales or service personnel whose duties do not require access to classified information;
- to maintenance or cleaning personnel who may only have inadvertent access to classified information unless such access cannot be reasonably prevented;
- to persons who perform maintenance on office equipment, computers, typewriters, and similar equipment who can be denied classified access by physical security measures;
- to perimeter security personnel who have no access to classified information; and
- to drivers, chauffeurs and food service personnel.

In addition, DOD's Under Secretary of Defense for Personnel and Readiness issued a memorandum requiring the use of OPM's position designation system and tool to determine the sensitivity level for civilian positions. Further, some of the DOD components that we visited have developed policies that extend beyond the DOD personnel security policy.

Army: Army officials affirmed that they use OPM's position designation tool to determine the sensitivity level of all civilian positions. In addition, Army Regulation 380-67 defines sensitive positions and gives heads of DOD components or their designees authority, subject to certain conditions, to delegate the designation of position sensitivity within their chain of command. Further, a 2006 Army memorandum called for sensitivity reviews of all Army civilian positions every 2 years, at a minimum.

Navy: According to officials, the Department of the Navy follows guidance in the Secretary of the Navy Regulation M-5510.30 along with DOD's personnel security regulation, which requires designators to set the clearance level for civilian personnel according to the risk the position poses. According to a Navy personnel security official, Human Resources offices and local commands have been revalidating positions according to the needs of the command in response to a 2011 memorandum from the

Assistant Secretary of the Navy for Manpower and Reserve Affairs. According to Navy officials, Human Resources offices used the position designation tool provided by OPM to determine the sensitivity level for all civilian positions.

Air Force: The Air Force uses Air Force Instruction 31-501 coupled with the DOD 5200.2-R to implement its personnel security program. According to the instruction, commanders with position designation authority determine the security sensitivity of civilian positions. Each position is coded with the appropriate security access requirement and identified in the unit manning document and the Defense Civilian Personnel Data System. If the security access requirement code requires a change, the unit commander submits an authorization change request to the servicing security activity. The commander also conducts an annual review of positions to determine the accuracy of position coding and adjust coding if necessary. Air Force officials confirmed that they are using OPM's Position Designation System and Tool to determine the proper sensitivity level for all civilian positions. Also, according to Air Force officials, in situations where a commander wants to upgrade a particular position, it must be reviewed and approved by a 3-star general.

Washington Headquarters Services: Washington Headquarters Services oversees position designation for certain DOD headquarters activities and defense agencies. According to Washington Headquarters Services officials, these agencies and activities follow DOD's personnel security regulation for position designation and use OPM's position designation system and tool in accordance with DOD policy.[2]

---

[2]See Washington Headquarters Services memorandum entitled *Implementation of the Position Designation Automated Tool* (Sept. 27, 2011).

Appendix III: Personnel Security Clearance Process

Since 1997, federal agencies have followed a common set of personnel security investigative standards and adjudicative guidelines for determining whether federal workers and others[1] are eligible to receive security clearances.[2] Once an applicant is selected for a position that requires a security clearance, government agencies rely on a multiphased personnel security clearance process that includes the application submission phase, investigation phase, and adjudication phase, among others. Different departments and agencies may have slightly different security clearance processes—the steps outlined below are intended to be illustrative of a typical process.

- The application submission phase. A security officer from an executive branch agency (1) requests an investigation of an individual requiring a clearance; (2) forwards a personnel security questionnaire (Standard Form 86) using the Office of Personnel Management's (OPM) e-QIP system or a paper copy of the Standard Form 86 to the individual to complete; (3) reviews the completed questionnaire; and (4) sends the questionnaire and supporting documentation, such as fingerprints and signed waivers, to OPM or the investigation service provider.
- The investigation phase. Federal investigative standards and OPM's internal guidance are typically used to conduct and document the investigation of the applicant. The scope of information gathered in an investigation depends on the level of clearance needed and whether the investigation is for an initial clearance or a reinvestigation for a clearance renewal. For example, in an investigation for a top secret clearance, investigators gather additional information through more time-consuming efforts, such as traveling to conduct in-person interviews to corroborate information about an applicant's employment and education. After the investigation is complete, the resulting investigative report is provided to the agency.

---

[1]Others include military servicemembers and private industry personnel; however, the scope of this report is federal civilian workers.

[2]Memorandum from Samuel Berger, Assistant to the President for National Security Affairs, to George J. Tenet and John P. White, Co-Chairmen, Security Policy Board, *Implementation of Executive Order 12968* (Mar. 24, 1997). This memorandum approves the adjudication guidelines, temporary eligibility standards, and investigative standards required by Executive Order 12968, *Access to Classified Information* (Aug. 2, 1995), as amended. The standards were later published in 32 C.F.R. Part 147. Further, the standards were updated in 2005; however, those updates are not currently reflected at 32 C.F.R. Part 147.

- The adjudication phase. Adjudicators from an agency use the information from the investigative report to determine whether an applicant is eligible for a security clearance. To make clearance eligibility decisions, the adjudication guidelines specify that adjudicators consider 13 specific areas that elicit information about (1) conduct that could raise security concerns and (2) factors that could allay those security concerns and permit granting a clearance.

In addition, once the background investigation and adjudication for a security clearance are complete, the requesting agency determines whether the individual is eligible for access to classified information. However, often the security clearance—either at the secret or top secret level—does not become effective until an individual needs to work with classified information. At that point, the individual would sign a nondisclosure agreement and receive a briefing in order for the clearance to become effective. DOD commonly employs this practice and, in some cases, the individual ultimately never requires access to classified information. Therefore, not all security clearance investigations result in an active security clearance.

Finally, once an individual is in a position that requires access to classified national security information, that individual is reinvestigated periodically at intervals that are dependent on the level of security clearance. For example, top secret clearanceholders are reinvestigated every 5 years, and secret clearanceholders are reinvestigated every 10 years.

Appendix IV: Comments from the Office of the Director of National Intelligence

JUL 0 3 2012

Ms. Brenda S. Farrell
Director
Defense Capabilities and Management
U.S. Government Accountability Office
Washington, DC 20548

Dear Ms. Farrell,

The Office of the Director of National Intelligence (ODNI) appreciates the opportunity to respond to the Government Accountability Office's (GAO) draft report, *Security Clearances: Agencies Need Clearly Defined Policy for Determining Civilian Position Requirements* (GAO-12-800).

The ODNI concurs with GAO's three formal recommendations for executive action. This report is a fair assessment of existing executive branch policies and procedures for determining security clearance requirements for federal civilian positions. We recognize that the emphasis of the report is on access to classified information. However, we wish to emphasize that the DNI's role as Security Executive Agent under Executive Order 13467 applies to all sensitive positions, of which sensitive positions requiring access to classified information is a narrower subset. Accordingly, guidance issued by the DNI as Security Executive Agent will cover all sensitive positions and associated investigative standards and adjudicative guidelines.

The enclosure provides the ODNI's detailed response to GAO's findings and recommendations. Again, thank you for the opportunity to comment. Please contact the ODNI/Office of Legislative Affairs at (703) 275-2457 if you have any questions.

Sincerely,

Kathleen Turner
Director of Legislative Affairs

Enclosure

Office of the Director of National Intelligence Response

GAO Draft Report: *Security Clearances: Agencies Need Clearly Defined Policy for Determining Civilian Position Requirements (GAO-12-800)*

GAO Recommendation 1: The GAO recommends that the Director of National Intelligence (DNI), in coordination with the Director of the Office of Personnel Management (OPM) and other executive branch agencies as appropriate, issue clearly-defined policy and procedures for federal agencies to follow when determining if federal civilian positions require a security clearance.

ODNI Response: Concur. The Office of the Director of National Intelligence (ODNI) agrees that executive branch agencies require simplified and uniform policy guidance to assist in determining appropriate sensitivity designations for all federal civilian positions across the Federal Government, which is foundational to determining the proper scope of investigation of any individual proposed to occupy the position. Indeed, the ODNI recognizes the need to issue such policy with respect to all sensitive positions as called out in Executive Order 13467, not just for sensitive positions that require access to classified information.

In the *Security and Suitability Process Reform Strategic Framework*, dated February 2010, a key reform deliverable identified for enhancing reciprocity is the consistent implementation of overarching policy guidance such as "position designation guidance that assists agencies in selecting the appropriate investigative level for their position." The ODNI and OPM are working toward achieving this deliverable by completing revisions to 5 CFR 732, which will result in the issuance of national level policy guidance on position sensitivity designations for certain categories of personnel across the Federal Government. Specifically, the ODNI is working with its reform partners (OPM, DoD, and OMB) on proposed revisions to the 732 language that describes the type of duties and responsibilities that shall be considered by agencies when making national security position designation decisions. With assistance from OMB, the ODNI and OPM expect to jointly issue the revised 732 language by the end of 2012. Further, because 5 CFR 732 does not apply to all categories of personnel across the Federal Government, the DNI, in his role as Security Executive Agent (SecEA), will separately issue guidance applicable to the remaining categories of personnel to achieve the greatest uniformity possible for sensitive position designations US Government-wide.

GAO Recommendation 2: The GAO recommends that, once policies and procedures are issued, the Director of National Intelligence and the Director of the OPM collaborate in their respective roles as executive agents to revise the positions designation tool to reflect that guidance.

ODNI Response: Concur. ODNI, in collaboration with OPM and other executive branch agencies, through the SecEA Advisory Committee, will develop a position designation tool that provides detailed descriptions of the types of positions where the occupant, due to the duties and responsibilities of the position, could bring about a material adverse impact to national security and thereby warrant a sensitive position designation. The ODNI believes that a tool that provides agencies with detailed descriptions of this type will bring about greater uniformity across the government in agency position sensitivity designations, which in turn will achieve consistency in the level of investigation performed on similarly situated individuals.

<u>Office of the Director of National Intelligence Response</u>

GAO Draft Report: *Security Clearances: Agencies Need Clearly Defined Policy for Determining Civilian Position Requirements* (GAO-12-800)

GAO Recommendation 3: The GAO recommends that the Director of National Intelligence, in coordination with the Director of the Office of Personnel Management (OPM) and other executive branch agencies as appropriate, issue guidance to require executive branch agencies to periodically review and revise or validate the designation of all federal civilian positions.

ODNI Response: Concur. The duties and responsibilities of federal civilian positions may be subject to change due to agency mission requirements or other emerging issues that will require an agency to reevaluate position sensitivity designations. ODNI will work with OPM and other executive branch agencies through the SecEA Advisory Committee to ensure that position designation policy and procedures include requirements for agencies to conduct periodic reviews of position designations to ensure the appropriate investigative coverage for each position.

Appendix V: Comments from the Office of Personnel Management

UNITED STATES OFFICE OF PERSONNEL MANAGEMENT
Washington, DC 20415

The Director

July 3, 2012

Brenda S. Farrell
Director, Defense Capabilities and Management
United States Government Accountability Office
441 G. Street. NW
Washington, DC 20548

Dear Ms. Farrell,

Thank you for providing the U.S. Office of Personnel Management (OPM) the opportunity to comment on the Government Accountability Office (GAO) draft report "Security Clearances: Agencies Need Clearly Defined Policy for Determining Civilian Position Requirements (GAO-12-800)." We appreciate GAO's time and effort throughout the review and the opportunity to respond to the draft report, to further support the good work already done by GAO.

There are three joint recommendations for the Director of National Intelligence (DNI) and the Director of OPM (which we have set out in the section below). OPM has organized its response into two additional sections – one dealing with the recommendations, in particular the second recommendation, which is addressed more directly to OPM, and one covering more technical points concerning areas of the report where additional clarification or information is needed.

Recommendations for Executive Action

"We recommend that the Director of National Intelligence, in coordination with the Director of OPM and other executive branch agencies as appropriate, issue clearly-defined policy and procedures for federal agencies to follow when determining if federal civilian positions require a security clearance.

In addition, we recommend that, once the policy and procedures are issued, the Director of National Intelligence and the Director of OPM collaborate in their respective roles as executive agents to revise the position designation tool to reflect that guidance.

Finally, we recommend that the Director of National Intelligence, in coordination with the Director of OPM and other executive branch agencies as appropriate, issue guidance to require executive branch agencies to periodically review and revise or validate the designation of all federal civilian positions."

OPM Response

We concur with the GAO recommendation to collaborate with the DNI (in our respective roles as executive agents) to revise the position designation tool. Indeed, we committed to do so in the "Security and Suitability Process Reform Strategic Framework" document of February 2010, which was executed by the Deputy Director for Management of the Office of Management and Budget, the

Director of OPM, the Under Secretary of Defense for Intelligence at the Department of Defense, and the Deputy Director of National Intelligence for Policy, Plans and Requirements. Revising the Position Designation Tool is listed as a future deliverable in this document (and expressly assigned to OPM). Id. at 6. OPM also noted, in publishing proposed revisions to 5 C.F.R. part 732, that following the "updates and clarifications" it intended to promulgate "OPM will issue further detailed guidance in its Position Designation System and other supplementary issuances." Logically, however, any revisions to the tool will need to await final action with respect to the proposed position designation regulations, which is still pending at this juncture.

The report touches upon two position designation processes. E.O. 10450 establishes that "[t]he appointment of each civilian officer or employee in any department or agency of the Government shall be made subject to investigation," id. at § 3(a); that in order to determine the appropriate scope of the investigation, "[t]he head of any department or agency shall designate, or cause to be designated, any position within his department or agency the occupant of which could bring about, by virtue of the nature of the position, a material adverse effect on the national security as a sensitive position," id. at § 3(b); and that "[t]he scope of the investigation shall be determined in the first instance according to the degree of adverse effect the occupant of the position sought to be filled could bring about, by virtue of the nature of the position, on the national security . . .," id. at § 3(a). E.O. 10450 makes OPM primarily responsible for the investigation of persons entering or employed in the competitive service. Id. at § 8(b). Accordingly, for positions in the competitive service, OPM, many years ago, promulgated regulations at 5 C.F.R. part 732 that prescribe levels of sensitivity (within the general category of sensitive positions) from which agencies must choose in performing a position designation under E.O. 10450. These designations permit OPM to perform the related background investigation at the appropriate scope.

In contrast, E.O. 10577, as amended, establishes that OPM is responsible for "[i]nvestigating the . . . suitability of applicants for positions in the competitive service." See Rule 5.2(a) of the Civil Service Rules, codified at 5 C.F.R. § 5.2(a). Pursuant to this presidential delegation of authority, OPM has promulgated 5 C.F.R. part 731, which establishes the rules governing the suitability process, including a requirement that "[a]gency heads must designate every covered position within the agency at a high, moderate, or low risk level as determined by the position's potential for adverse impact to the efficiency or integrity of the service." 5 C.F.R. § 731.106(a). (We note that section 731.106(a) also touches upon the position designation tool: "OPM will provide an example of a risk designation system for agency use in an OPM issuance . . . .".) In this scheme, the designations once again permit OPM to determine the appropriate scope of the background investigation. See 5 C.F.R. § 731.106(c). In addition, they permit the suitability adjudicator – either OPM or an agency exercising adjudicative authority pursuant to a delegation from OPM, depending upon the context (see 5 C.F.R. § 731.105) – to view conduct and character issues developed in the resulting background investigation through the prism of the position's potential for adverse impact to the efficiency or integrity of the service.

Properly functioning position designation processes are thus fundamental to correctly adjudicating whether an individual's appointment is "clearly consistent with the interests of the national security" (in accordance with E.O. 10450, sec. 2) and whether an individual is suitable for appointment to or retention in the competitive service (in accordance with part 731).   The position designation tool was designed to help agencies with these processes by providing guidance relating to both in a unified document. OPM will be pleased to consult with the DNI on appropriate changes to the position designation tool once the proposed changes to the existing regulations are resolved. In the interim, agencies may find the reasoning in the proposed regulations themselves, and the supplementary information, a helpful resource in making position designations within the national security scheme.

OPM also would be pleased to work with the DNI on guidance concerning periodic reviews of existing designations (the third recommendation), once pending proposed regulations are finalized. With respect to the first recommendation, however, it is not clear to OPM that it has a significant role in prescribing the policy and procedures for federal agencies to follow when determining if federal civilian positions require a security clearance. Executive Order 12968, as amended by E.O. 13467, gives agency heads the ultimate responsibility to grant or deny security clearances, subject to investigative standards and adjudicative guidelines prescribed by the DNI, not by OPM. Because OPM has the primary responsibility to conduct security clearance investigation for Federal civilian and contract employment and for service in the Armed Forces, however, OPM would be willing to engage with the DNI and other agencies with respect to aspects of such policy and procedures that deal with the investigative process itself.

Additional Points for Consideration

One of the premises upon which this report is based is not accurate, and thus detracts from the cogency of GAO's observations. GAO repeatedly posits that agencies must perform the national security position designation in order to know whether the occupant will require a security clearance. See, e.g., p. 2 ("Determining the requirements of a federal position includes assessing both the risk and sensitivity level associated with a position to inform whether that position requires a security clearance"); p. 3 ("According to OPM, positions that an agency designates as special-sensitive and critical-sensitive require a background investigation that typically results in a top secret clearance"); p. 5 ("The personnel security clearance process begins when a human resources or security professional determines a position's level of sensitivity, which informs whether or not a position requires a security clearance . . ."); and p. 12 ("According to OPM and ODNI officials, the purpose of the revision is to clarify and broaden the standards for designating whether federal positions are national security sensitive, which will help agencies more accurately assess the sensitivity of a position, which then indicates whether a position requires a security clearance and the level of clearance").

The way the process works, however, is the other way around. Whether the occupant of a particular position will need access to classified information or eligibility for such access (i.e., a security clearance) is one of the factors that help determine whether a position is sensitive. Accordingly, an agency should first determine whether the occupant of a given position will need access to classified information, and, if so, at what level, before attempting to designate a position in the national security scheme. The standard is set out in E.O. 12968 § 2.1(2) ("Except in agencies where eligibility for access is a mandatory condition of employment, eligibility for access to classified information shall only be requested or granted based on a demonstrated, foreseeable need for access. Requesting or approving eligibility in excess of actual requirements is prohibited."). If the occupant will need "regular use of, or access to, classified information," the position is automatically deemed sensitive. 5 C.F.R. § 732.102(2). If the occupant does not have a demonstrated, foreseeable need for such access, the agency must then consider an alternative factor – whether the position is one of those that "involve activities of the Government that are concerned with the protection of the nation from foreign aggression or espionage, including development of defense plans or policies, intelligence or counterintelligence activities, and related activities concerned with the preservation of the military strength of the United States . . . ." Id. at § 732.102(1).

Accordingly, there is no basis for GAO to conclude that OPM's position designation tool affects how agencies determine whether the occupant of a position requires access to classified information or eligibility for such access.

We provided GAO with copies of audits we performed on agencies that employ competitive service civilian personnel, and we noted inconsistencies in agency applications of the tool. In assessing whether OPM's position designation tool played any role in such inconsistencies, it is important to note that effective use of OPM's "tool" requires three pre-conditions. First, the individual using the tool must be knowledgeable about the relevant factors and trained in the discernment processes per OPM's instructions. Second, in each scheme, proper designation requires position information from various sources, including the Position Description (PD), the supervisor, and security and human resource personnel. A PD alone will rarely provide enough information to assess the risk and sensitivity of a position. Third, the position designation process will be successful only if the tool is applied as developed, without overriding or supplemental instruction from the employing agency which may alter tool results. The overriding agency supplemental instructions that GAO noted were in place at DHS and DoD may well have contributed to the inconsistent results GAO observed. Our audits show that in agencies where these conditions were met, the tool was effective and consistent. OPM's current guidance sets forth these conditions for the agencies' consideration.

As cited by this report, OPM worked with agencies under the Springer-Hadley initiative to simplify and streamline the two position designation processes. In meetings with subject matter experts from the Department of Defense (DoD) and the Department of Homeland Security (DHS), it was not suggested to us that our tool required more detail or direction with respect to the security clearance process. In any event, as noted above, OPM has no special interpretive role to play with respect to determining which positions require security clearances.

We also take this opportunity to address GAO's observation that the amount of material devoted to the suitability designation process seemed out of proportion with the amount of material devoted to the designation process for national security sensitivity. OPM notes that, for sensitive positions, the position designation tool focused principally on the level of security clearance required, a standard which is prescribed by Executive order. However, OPM provided relatively few details about the appropriate designation of sensitive positions in which the incumbent does not require a security clearance. Our proposed revision of 5 C.F.R. part 732 was intended to establish a basis for more detailed guidance, as noted in the accompanying Federal Register notice.

We stand ready to collaborate with the DNI as appropriate on the GAO recommendations.

Sincerely,

John Berry
Director

Appendix VI: Comments from the Department of Homeland Security

U.S. Department of Homeland Security
Washington, DC 20528

July 3, 2012

Brenda S. Farrell
Director, Defense Capabilities and Management
U.S. Government Accountability Office
441 G Street, NW
Washington, DC 20548

Re: Draft Report GAO-12-800, "SECURITY CLEARANCES: Agencies Need Clearly
        Defined Policy for Determining Civilian Position Requirements"

Dear Ms. Farrell:

Thank you for the opportunity to review and comment on this draft report. The U.S. Department
of Homeland Security (DHS) appreciates the U.S. Government Accountability Office's (GAO)
work in conducting its review and issuing this report.

The Department is pleased to note GAO's positive acknowledgement of DHS' efforts to ensure
only those who need a security clearance are authorized one. For example, DHS conducts
periodic Security Compliance Reviews which evaluate individual component personnel security
programs throughout the Department, and include an evaluation of the investigations conducted
compared to the position sensitivity level of individual positions.

Although the report does not contain any recommendations specifically directed to DHS, the
Department remains committed to being an active member of the government wide Suitability
and Security Clearance Performance Accountability Council. This includes helping look at
security reform issues and implementing Joint Reform Team initiatives, as appropriate.

Again, thank you for the opportunity to review and comment on this draft report. Please feel free
to contact me if you have any questions. We look forward to working with you in the future.

Sincerely,

Jim H. Crumpacker
Director
Departmental GAO-OIG Liaison Office

Appendix VII: GAO Contact and Staff Acknowledgments

GAO Contact	Brenda S. Farrell, (202) 512-3604 or farrellb@gao.gov
Staff Acknowledgments	In addition to the contact named above, David Moser (Assistant Director), Sara Cradic, Cynthia Grant, Nicole Harris, Jeffrey Heit, Kimberly Mayo, Richard Powelson, Jason Wildhagen, Michael Willems, and Elizabeth Wood made key contributions to this report.

Related GAO Products

Personnel Security Clearances: Continuing Leadership and Attention Can Enhance Momentum Gained from Reform Effort. GAO-12-815T. Washington, D.C.: June 21, 2012.

Background Investigations: Office of Personnel Management Needs to Improve Transparency of Its Pricing and Seek Cost Savings. GAO-12-197. Washington, D.C.: February 28, 2012.

High-Risk Series: An Update. GAO-11-278. Washington, D.C.: February 2011.

Personnel Security Clearances: Overall Progress Has Been Made to Reform the Governmentwide Security Clearance Process. GAO-11-232T. Washington, D.C.: December 1, 2010.

Personnel Security Clearances: Progress Has Been Made to Improve Timeliness but Continued Oversight Is Needed to Sustain Momentum. GAO-11-65. Washington, D.C.: November 19, 2010.

DOD Personnel Security Clearance Reform: Preliminary Observations on Timeliness and Quality. GAO-11-185T. Washington, D.C.: November 16, 2010.

Privacy: OPM Should Better Monitor Implementation of Privacy-Related Policies and Procedures for Background Investigations. GAO-10-849. Washington, D.C.: September 7, 2010.

Personnel Security Clearances: An Outcome-Focused Strategy and Comprehensive Reporting of Timeliness and Quality Would Provide Greater Visibility over the Clearance Process. GAO-10-117T. Washington, D.C.: October 1, 2009.

Personnel Security Clearances: Progress Has Been Made to Reduce Delays but Further Actions Are Needed to Enhance Quality and Sustain Reform Efforts. GAO-09-684T. Washington, D.C.: September 15, 2009.

Personnel Security Clearances: An Outcome-Focused Strategy Is Needed to Guide Implementation of the Reformed Clearance Process. GAO-09-488. Washington, D.C.: May 19, 2009.

DOD Personnel Clearances: Comprehensive Timeliness Reporting, Complete Clearance Documentation, and Quality Measures Are Needed to Further Improve the Clearance Process. GAO-09-400. Washington, D.C.: May 19, 2009.

High-Risk Series: An Update. GAO-09-271. Washington, D.C.: January 22, 2009.

DOD Personnel Clearances: Preliminary Observations about Timeliness and Quality. GAO-09-261R. Washington, D.C.: December 19, 2008.

Personnel Security Clearances: Preliminary Observations on Joint Reform Efforts to Improve the Governmentwide Clearance Eligibility Process. GAO-08-1050T. Washington, D.C.: July 30, 2008.

Personnel Clearances: Questions for the Record Regarding Security Clearance Reform. GAO-08-965R. Washington, D.C.: July 14, 2008.

Personnel Clearances: Key Factors for Reforming the Security Clearance Process. GAO-08-776T. Washington, D.C.: May 22, 2008.

Employee Security: Implementation of Identification Cards and DOD's Personnel Security Clearance Program Need Improvement. GAO-08-551T. Washington, D.C.: April 9, 2008.

DOD Personnel Clearances: Questions for the Record Related to the Quality and Timeliness of Clearances. GAO-08-580R. Washington D.C.: March 25, 2008.

DOD Personnel Clearances: DOD Faces Multiple Challenges in Its Efforts to Improve Clearance Processes for Industry Personnel. GAO-08-470T. Washington, D.C.: February 12, 2008.

Personnel Clearances: Key Factors to Consider in Efforts to Reform Security Clearance Processes. GAO-08-352T. Washington, D.C.: February 27, 2008.

DOD Personnel Clearances: Improved Annual Reporting Would Enable More Informed Congressional Oversight. GAO-08-350. Washington, D.C.: February 13, 2008.

DOD Personnel Clearances: Delays and Inadequate Documentation Found for Industry Personnel. GAO-07-842T. Washington, D.C.: May 17, 2007.

High Risk Series: An Update. GAO-07-310. Washington, D.C.: January 2007.

DOD Personnel Clearances: Additional OMB Actions Are Needed to Improve the Security Clearance Process. GAO-06-1070. Washington, D.C.: September 28, 2006.

DOD Personnel Clearances: Questions and Answers for the Record Following the Second in a Series of Hearings on Fixing the Security Clearance Process. GAO-06-693R. Washington, D.C.: June 14, 2006.

DOD Personnel Clearances: New Concerns Slow Processing of Clearances for Industry Personnel. GAO-06-748T. Washington, D.C.: May 17, 2006.

DOD Personnel Clearances: Funding Challenges and Other Impediments Slow Clearances for Industry Personnel. GAO-06-747T. Washington, D.C.: May 17, 2006.

Questions for the Record Related to DOD's Personnel Security Clearance Program and the Government Plan for Improving the Clearance Process. GAO-06-323R. Washington, D.C.: January 17, 2006.

DOD Personnel Clearances: Government Plan Addresses Some Long-standing Problems with DOD's Program, But Concerns Remain. GAO-06-233T. Washington, D.C.: November 9, 2005.

DOD Personnel Clearances: Some Progress Has Been Made but Hurdles Remain to Overcome the Challenges That Led to GAO's High-Risk Designation. GAO-05-842T. Washington, D.C.: June 28, 2005.

High-Risk Series: An Update. GAO-05-207. Washington, D.C.: January 2005.

www.ingramcontent.com/pod-product-compliance
Lightning Source LLC
Chambersburg PA
CBHW080909290526
45795CB00007BA/2466